THE

ANGEL
ORACLE

BOOK

NEYAH

NEYAH
THE ANGEL ORACLE BOOK

Artwork by : Riccardo Giuffrè

Foreword

This oracle book was entirely channeled from the angelic group Ray and it is a guidance to reconnect all of you to the true essence of who you really are :

Love

Instructions

This book comes with no instructions,
there isn't a right or wrong way to use it.
There is simply your way.
You can use it daily, for guidance.
You can close your eyes and ask your
angels for the message you need to hear.
You could even rip off the pages and
create your oracle deck with them.
There is only your way.
Expand and create, because

You are the Oracle

Enlightenment is your greatest gift.

All your actions echo through eternity.

Every step you take is always one step closer towards your light.

Find love where everybody else is afraid
to find it and there you'll find your truth.

The beginning is only the first step in your endless unfoldment in the endless spiral of your journey.

I can see your light, therefore, you can see yours and you can remember the light to others.

Every concern you have is understandable and it's been heard. But remember, you have all the time that you need, so stop worrying.

I am an incredible unlimited being and my beauty is my unique essence that shines from within.

I am the strength that carries on in the middle of the storm, remember your power.

Love is your wellness, love is your experience.

Stop denying the truth, because your soul is sending you the messages you're trying to hide from yourself. Listen.

We are here now and We'll be here in eternity. Call upon us in times of need and be always open to receive.

There is beauty in what you call uncertainty too. Beauty is in the process of creating your own experience. Enjoy the process with eagerness, enjoy.

Love is an eternal bond, once it is established, it carries on through eternity.

Souls that joy as one in love are the
living example of heaven on earth.

Blessings arrive.

It's always the time to remember your dreams and follow them through. Because nobody can make them happen the way that you can.

We are abundant, because we never forget who we were and who we are.

Remembering the nature of your existence will fill yourself with great miracles and abundance.

Find the answers questioning things
without fear in your heart.

Water can purify your soul. Water has a consciousness of his own. It has memory. It is life. Use water, allow water to fill you with its wisdom.

The earthly nature has something to tell you, go out and listen, don't be afraid to connect to your mother's womb.

All the ancient sage and wise ones found the answers to a quiet and still mind. Do you think you'll be able to find your answer in such a troubled mind? Learn from those who came before you and practice stillness.

Seeing the interconnection of all things, of all creatures, is the blessing of this earth.

My awareness makes me eager to create more with my time and I appreciate the possibilities of my vast creation.

You're never alone, you never were and never you'll be.

Peace is the only state from which I begin to create. With no peace, I'd rather stay quiet. There is no creation without a peaceful intention and a peaceful mind.

Love will always find you. Open up yourself to the possibility of experiencing what you call love and they will always find you.

Many things have been stored in your consciousness, many things from the past, many encounters from lost times. But nothing in you is ever lost. We just find each other again and again until we're whole and complete.

Sometimes you wonder where home is. Look at the sky and look within you, you are home.

I have been many but I'm one.

Sometimes the answer must be no.

Everything will be revealed when the time calls for it. Trust.

Everybody carries some heavy luggage on their shoulders. Pain is a heavy emotion. It wears your spine and enables you to love again. We understand you, but we invite you to connect better. Pain can always be released and love can always be found. Because it was never lost in the first place.

You didn't come here to determine what's possible and what's not. You just came here to do it.
Let us decide what's possible and what's not. Don't limit yourself and do it.

There's no dream too big for us and for you.

Your purpose is to live, create and experience in all the spectrum of this human existence. Being obsessed over a purpose will only trap you in your own mind. Do what you love and your purpose will find you.

We see many challenges and we understand their difficulties. But we always see you overcoming them and you will. Believe that you will.

You're like a child that we love and support. Would you ever tell a child that he cannot fulfill his desires? Talk to yourself like you were that child and start the conversation again. We assure you'll notice a big difference.

Every soul longs for a creative expression. Creativity is one the great gifts of this existence because it allows you to vision your greatest possibilities. Live your life creatively and your life will create itself.

At times some will deny their true nature in the form of lies in authenticity or dishonesty. Some part of you will feel angry. You have a choice. You can feed anger or remember they just forgot who they are and leave them. Lead yourself example, choose your authenticity and they will choose it through you.

I am amazed by the wonderful possibilities of this life. I can see everyday hidden blessings.

Say yes to yourself, say yes.

Your decisions are bold and assertive. Be proud, you came a long way.

Among all the things you did in your life, which is the one you cherish the most about? Sometimes remembering is good for the heart. Because it takes you back to a place or a time when you loved, felt loved or both.

There is an endless stream of energy that connects all things in the universe, like a cosmic dance under an outstanding melody. Can you hear it? Can you feel it? Can you see it? It's there for you too.

You are aware. Every time you are aware of your being, of your presence, of your body, of this existence, it's a time to celebrate. You don't need any special reason than this to celebrate life.

The moon and its faces help me understand the cycle of life. My life is like a river. It branches all off, as an extension of a greater source. And I'm like the river, made by the same elements of that source. And I'm never like the river, separated from my source.

Love is a wonderful feeling. When it's reciprocated and natural between two souls, it's a great gift on this earth.

I am beyond what I can see, but I
appreciate what I see.

A mind that wonders is always a mind that's capable to imagine greater visions. You are an all knowing creature and what you know now may be different from what someone else knows now as well. But it's perfect for both of you.

You can make the difference everyday.
Not necessarily with greater gestures.
But in your daily life, in your daily
activities, through a kind word, through
a truthful advice, through a loving
thought, you are making the difference.

Crystals store great wisdom from the earth. You are allowed to connect and use them for your own and others' good. Pick a crystal today and bring it in your tomorrow.

The very fact that you woke up
breathing, able to feel the fresh breeze of
the morning, it's a reason to celebrate.
And when the people you love woke up
too, then it's an incredible day.

From this point you can start and appreciate your experience each and every day. And we'll remain here in Love to support you always.

By closing your eyes and opening your mind I am capable to receive all the answers you are seeking. And I am able to see others through the eye of your inner awareness.

As you focus on what you want, we will give you ideas, inspiration to take the right actions and will align to people that will be important on your journey.

You are called to lead your life.

Harmony within will influence and propel more and more harmonious relationships outside yourself. Try to find your own balance, without being a pendulum that swifts from an emotion to another.
We fully understand that, at times, it can be exciting to try some roller coasters.
But in the long term we know that harmony and balance are the products of peace. Where there is peace there is Love, that is who you naturally are.

It's important to take a break sometimes and take care of your heart, mind and body. This vehicle is a precious temple, enjoy this day, relax and give yourself care. Take it easy, smile and have fun with respect of your body. Wonderful things await you and today it's time to let go and enjoy.

When you understand the balance
between giving and receiving, you
understand a basic law of the universe.
When your kind words to others are
sincere you receive kindness back. When
your loving energy is shared in your
authenticity you also receive love. If you
don't feel to say any kind of loving
words, don't feel guilty. Ask yourself
why. It is better to reflect and stay in the
stillness rather than give words or
actions that your soul will later regret.
Because no action of hate or fear will
ever give you back Love, peace and
harmony.

When your heart is open to the truth of who you are, you're able to live a fulfilling experience. Because you're capable to become honest with yourself and others. And what a gift is this existence, when you can share your essence with others?

Everything you desire we heard. It's already yours.
Let go of control and allow our light to shower you with joy.
Patience is a great quality because it allows you to enjoy the wait as a fulfilling experience rather than a lacking experience.
Because a light being isn't and will never be a lacking being.

Time is an interesting concept. We can either talk about time as days in a calendar or see time as the experience we cherish for our expansion. And when you celebrate time in a non-linear frame you can truly absorb the lessons of its wisdom within you.

At times, some will leave your experience for a while or for this life. We understand your pain.
In us and in Source there's always great love for you. Because we know that nobody is ever lost or ever gone, we know they'll always be with you and with us, in great love and union. Accept the changes that this human experience presents you. Accept your feelings and let them go. Give them to us, so we can heal them and walk together with you in the next chapter of your life.

When you feel that your ego self is better than anybody else around you, we know you are choosing fear. When you see in others what you once felt, show compassion and care, we'll know that you have chosen yourself, the divine and true love.

I am a powerful light.

I experience life magic.

When you ask you always receive.

One day at a time I'm closer to the experiences I choose for myself. I'm thrilled to see what life has in store for me.

I enjoy one day at a time each and every step of this process.

If you ever walk in darkness, don't be afraid. We'll be here. Your light is always present. You simply forgot. There's no need to worry now that you remember. Light always outshines darkness.

Light guides you where you're meant to be.

Even when you're capable of great empathy and loving acts we don't want you to forget yourself. Respect your energy and meet yourself at the level that you're at. You can help others. But you will help them more once you set some loving healthy boundaries.

You are a Divine Sacred being. That's how we see you. Don't forget that.

When I allow myself to open my heart chakra I'm able to give myself love and send this love also to the ones I care. In every moment I can choose love rather than fear.

Writing down, even to us, what you'd like to experience, brings you closer to your divine nature and to the manifestations of your own desires. Write and have fun envisioning your dreams.

There's no need to be so harsh on yourself. Life is never a failure, rather a great unfoldment. What you perceive as a failure today, will be the blessing of your tomorrow. Try again, don't lose hope, you are only expanding.

It's okay to ask and seek the help of others in times of need, when you don't feel at your best, or capable to handle life the way you want. Don't be afraid, there's great courage in asking a loving hand for help.

Everything you do is a teaching to others
and others are always teaching to you.
It's a great cosmic exchange.

I see the lessons of my life and I thank the people that were involved in those lesson. I let go of pain because I understood, through that contrast, who I am and where I am going. I let go of regrets. I understand and I'm able to forgive. And when I forgive, I get one step closer to Love and to my inner essence.

When I love, I love unconditionally. Because I know that love under conditions is too tight of a box to fit more than one soul.

When you let people be free to be who they are, you're allowing yourself that permission too, and you're able to walk together with another being in Love under no rules and any set of conditions.

Take your time, there is no rush.

You're never worried about money, work or prosperity. You're worried about the feelings of lack, of prosperity. Because those things are neither bad or good in essence, but they're connected to your desires of safety, joy and freedom. But you are safe. You can choose joy. You are a free being. Align yourself to those truths and the rest will align for you.

I believe in miracles because I am a miracle divine creation.

I am a creator and I'm able to create and experience miracles.

When you know who you are, you're capable of acceptance. Talk to yourself, meditate, discover your wonderful transcendental universe. And you will discover the Divine.

Breathe in and breathe out. It's all it takes to feel. Breathe in and breathe out.

Nothing is impossible. The only limit I have are the ones I impose on myself.

It doesn't need to open any gate or portal to talk to Angels. It doesn't need any certificate or supernatural gift. We are here and we can hear you. We know how to give you signs and messages. The only thing you have to do is talk to us from your heart. And listen with your heart. It could be a song, a bird singing, a butterfly crossing your sight or a number on your screen. Just pay attention and listen to your heart. We are here guiding you.

I listen to my body and respect what my body is telling me. My body and my soul together are my greater awareness.

Negative energy can always be transformed into positive. We can help you with that at any time. Every time you feel a negative feeling, ask yourself why, heal it with us and release it. So together we can visualize a positive outcome and transform negativity into a greater experience.

Healing is an important step. Because this human experience is a challenging process. Healing wounds and emotions is an healthy way to understand lessons, forgive and connect back to your true essence and purpose. There is nothing that cannot be healed by heavens' light.

You are safe.

I allow to receive intuitions from my inner guding system. I trust and listen to my intuitions.

There is beauty around you, provided through Earth, another living being, a wonderful consciousness on its own. Experience earth's beauty, and it will mirror back to you, your beauty too.

I understand that relationships are an important factor in my unfoldment. I appreciate time alone but I also cherish the moment with others around me. I align myself to experience healthy relationships in my life, filled with joy, grace and uplifting growing experiences.

When I become my own best friend I
attract friends that are the best for me.

I love you.

Eternal Love.

Music speaks the language of the Universe which is vibrations. When you live your blessings with an open heart, your vibrations become the harmonious rhythm that influences others to dance at the same beat.

Give yourself a chance. Give your dreams a chance. Give your relationship a chance. Sometimes it is asked to take a leap of faith, and only later you'll be able to see the rewards of that jump into the unknown. But your courage will strengthen your faith. And You will not regret following Love and your dreams.

Nothing is impossible for those who believe.

Balancing all your chakras, from the root to the crown and above, allows you to live a more balanced and healthier life. Integrating your earthly aspects with the connection to the higher realm. Practice meditation to improve, open and balance all your 7 chakras.

Share your truth without fear but only love in your heart. But don't forget to listen to others as well, because in the middle you will disover a new truth. Only those who remain open, live a life of wonders.

Forgive and learn. There's always a chance to forgive and forgiveness brings a new awareness to your experience, see the gift in all of them.

Healing cannot happen if you see yourself or others as damaged, sick, or wounded. Healing happens when you're willing to see yourself as we do. Healthy, Loving and Without Guilt. We will always support you on your healing everytime you need and everytime one of your loved ones will too.

We always have your back.

Thank you. Those are very important words.

Allow your heart and soul to sing with joy.

Great news will come your way soon.

Try again. What is that you're truly asking for? Is this necessary for your highest good?

Presence is the shortcut to enlightenment. There's no moment that is more important that NOW. Allow yourself to be present. You'll be suprised by how much you can learn from the wisdom of silence.

Change is an essential part of existence. Accepting change, even when unexpected, means understanding the blessings of all things and allowing the soul to evolve and grow. Embrace change.

There is great value in humility.
Recognize your talents and strengths but
don't cultivate your ego because of them.
Stay humble and you will climb
mountains with grace.

There is someone in heaven sending you
love to you now.

See the world through the lenses of your inner child. How much magic were you forgetting? Allow your immagination to shine through infinite possibilities.

Everything will be revealed to you. Of the informations that we'll give you, there is none that you aren't ready to handle.

Follow your visions and intuitions. They are guiding you on your divine path.

Shift the awareness on how you feel. So you'll be able to make conscious decisions in your life.

Connection is essential. Connection to your inner being, to Source and to others.

Listen to the Elements of Mother Earth. What is the sound of the wind telling you, what is water reflecting upon you, what is the fire calling within you? And what is the earth calling you to do?

There is great wisdom in simple things.
Love is simple. And so life can be.

When you clean and tidy up your physical space, you also make order in your mind. It's time to let go of old energy that's leaking your emotional body. Patch those leaks by cleaning your space and by making a list of all the things you know you're not going to do. That needs to be released, things from the past, lost hopes and old dreams. So the energy can be recycled and get back to you stronger than before. Everytime you make space away from the old you open your arms to recieve the blessings of the new.

Clearly decide what you want so it can manifest for you. It's time to make a decision.

Pay attention to your dreams. Keeping a dream journal and taking note of the messages you're receiving from your dreams is very important at this time.

Give to us, your angels, all your worries. So you can feel light and harmonious again. When you free yourself from anxiety and concerns, you're able to find and see the solutions that are present for you.

You already won.

I am Abundance.
I am Joy.
I am Love.

Your connection to books or creative writing is very important for you now. Read books that resonate with your higher vibrations or write down your feelings and thoughts in a journal. All of this will inspire you, your next moves.

We have infinite inspiration for you.
Seek for us, your Angels, within you,
and we will shower you with abundant
inspiration for your projects and life
path.

Prayers are not a way to worship the Divine. In heaven we need no worship. Prayers are natural communion with Source. You can pray, meditate or simply connect with your crown chakra to the higher realm. Prayers can purify your spirit from moments of confusion and negativity, they can release your pain and get you closer with Love allowing yourself to be open to receive.

Exercises are a fun and natural way to move your body and raise your vibration. Practice Yoga or other types of body work that will help you daily, to have more energy and a healthy mind and body. You will see great results, not only within yourself but also in your future manifestations.

Explore and Expand. There is so much to gain from allowing the new to come. Words don't teach, but experience does.

Focus on your priorities.

I allow myself to feel love and I easily express love to others. I treat myself with kindness and I notice this feeling around me today. The more I find it within me, the more Love finds me.

Your higher self is wise beyond your conscious understanding. Have fun connecting with it, researching and studying all the subjects you're passionate about. It's always a good day to learn and expand.

I allow myself to sing without judging myself, simply to give voice to my voice. I am my favourite music.

Dance to the rhythm of life. Dance and be in the flow.

You don't need to seek anything to run towards things. Align with who you are and things, people and experiences will come to you.

Buy a ring today or plant a seed in the ground. As a symbol of your commitment to life, to your dreams, to Love, and to yourself and the Divine. We are working with you to make that seed grow like your dreams. And to make you blossom at your fullest potential.

You are enough.

Slow down.
How many times you always wanted to
rush things?
Rushing into a relationship.
Rushing to get things done.
Rushing for the outcomes.
Slow down and breathe.
Isn't it wonderful to enjoy the now?

Let your eyes dream even when you're awake.

You are worthy.

Your desires are coming. Be grateful because they're coming to you now.

Use your emotions in a creative way.
Every emotion, even negative ones, can
be turned into Art. And when emotions
become Art they expand and fill the
heart of All.

Pay attention to your thoughts. You cannot have the manifestations that you want if you're at the same time afraid to recieve them. Ask to us, your angels, to help you remove any blockages that are limiting your experience.

Let go of Fear.

Use essential oils, like rose oil, to help you connect with the angels and with Love. There is great wisdom in the plants of this earth and in their fragrances, in their essence. You can also bring roses or other flowers in your home so that their energy and smell can empower you and connect you to love.

Animals are the keepers of this Earth. And you can learn so much from them. Connect to the Animal kingdom, be present with your pets, give thanks to those creatures, they are constantly connected to heaven. And so you can be.

Look at the sunset. Walk and soak the last glimpse of daylight. What do you feel?

Keep your word. It'll help you be more self-confident and give more respect to others. When you keep your words and you're correct to others, the Universe will do the same to you.

Forgive yourself, you didn't do anything
wrong.

Soul companions and Soul family are important in your unfoldment. Your soul is already whole and complete, but learning together and connecting through the vibration of your soul to another being is a wonderful feeling. It is what we call a family of Love.

Transform your anger into healing through forgiveness.

You deserve love and you're always loved. Don't forget it.

Make a list or a vision board of all the things you'd love to experience.
Make it fun, don't overthink it too much, just do it and choose what connects with you on a deeper level. Put the list or the board in a place where you can often see it. Those dreams speak to you daily, they are part of you.

Remember, at times, when you
experienced Love.

The only validation you need is yours. Stop seeking it from others. Everybody will have a different perception of yourself because everyone else can only see from the lenses of their own subjective self. The only person that knows you better than anybody else does, is YOU.

Don't forget to smile because it is contagious.

I can always choose at any time. And my future is the byproduct of my conscious choices.

I choose happiness now.

It is time to celebrate your hardwork.
Give yourself a gift.

We see your value and we invite you to see your value too. See the beauty of your being and allow yourself to see value and beauty in others. We are all one.

If you feel nobody understands you, it's simply your fear-based ego telling you that. We angels can understand you and we will align you with people that resonate with you and give you their total loving understanding.

Life doesn't happen to you but for you.
When you shift your perspective from
the victim role to your own Rescuer role,
you become, through responsibility, your
greatest Hero.

Let your light shine. When you express your true self your light shines, creating joy in yourself and others, through your own unique creative expressions. Use your light to guide and inspire others.

You are very sensitive to the energy of others and harsh emotions and situations. Life can be intense. Honour your sensitivity because it allows you to be empathic and compassionate towards others and feel every emotion intensely. It is a gift, not a curse.

Resolve conflicts finding a peaceful
resolution for all the parties involved.

When you're feeling insecure you're disconnected to Source, that has the highest image of you.
Connect to wellness and you'll heal your insecurities.
The only limit is your belief. Stop believing and start being.

Don't give up.

Pay attention to people that hide beyond masks. They forgot who they really are. Walk away from toxic people or situations with forgiveness in your heart.

Make plans, and work towards them daily with joy, passion and patience. Your hard work will be recognized.

You are a rich abundant being.

When I commit to a project I make sure to finish it, and that gives me great joy for all my accomplishments.

Everytime you're judging somebody you're automatically judging the false part of theirselves and so yours too. Judgement doesn't serve anybody, because it only reinforces the illusionary nature of the ego and all of its construct. Choose love.

You are a powerful lightworker. You always give a lot to others. Don't forget to rest sometimes. When you rest, you're able to recharge your energies and go back yo your work later with a greater light.

Be Grateful.

Celebrate your achievements. We see all of them and we congratulate with you for all that you've accomplished. Do the same today to you.

Make a wish, what is it that you truly want? Now stop wishing for it and Choose it.

Make room for Love, not for dramas.

You can bring the Divine in everything you do and connect to Source that creates universes, at any given time. You're an antenna giving the vibration of joy and Source responds with more joy and Love back to you.

Take the steps that are necessary for Love to blossom. We're giving you signs and synchronicities so you'll know which steps to take. Just Listen and recieve.

You already found what you need.

Even if humans get irritated by the concept of Divine Timing, we are here to tell you! Divine Timing is at work in your life right now! Trust, Heaven loves you.

You're carrying the past like a heavy closet on your shoulders, with all the memories in it.
Leave the closet home, you can open it when you need, but there's no need to carry it around your path like a heavy load. Set yourself free.

Explore new possibilities.

Trust. Faith in the Divine, The Angels and yourself are your greater strenght.

Let go.

Love is who you naturally are.

Everyday is a day towards the unfoldment of my life purpose. I walk my path with eagerness and excitement.

Soul expansion. You're not depressed. You're simply expanding. This is a great time to grow spiritually. Be gentle with yourself, we recognize your value. Things will improve.

Look at yourself and at others with the eyes of Source. What do you see?

It is not possible for you to experience what isn't your essence in vibrations. Your contradictions in how you feel are what is causing the distress that is occuring. Breathe. We understand. The only thing you have to do is focus back on your values, vibrational alignment and true essence.

There is nothing you can't do. A belief is only a thought that you keep repeating. What thought do you want to choose today?

You're a musical instrument emanating vibrations throughout the cosmo. And your music is the music you decide to play with your instrument, that is your mind, body and soul. Harmonious music is the language of the Universe.

Embrace the oneness of who you are.

A soul is a multidimensional unlimited being. Your soul is simply too complete, too vast, to fit in a limited box.

Did you remember to smile today? You are loved.

The best relationships are the ones where souls encounter each other in vibrational harmonics. Creating new music of Love for the planet.

Alignment is your greatest friend and opportunity.

Everything will be fine.

Opportunities are always coming, it is your job to recognize them and grasp them when the time is presented.

There is always light at the end of an experience.
There is always light within you and within everyone.

Look at the stars above you at night. You are part of the whole. And you're made by the same elements of stars.

Capture this moment and cherish about it in your heart for eternity. Love is eternal.

Making peace with the now is what brings you greater blessings in your tomorrow.

When you praise the abundance in others, you're praising abundance in you. We're not separate from each other and from all that is. Be brave! You're never wrong when you follow Love.

22398283R00244

Printed in Great Britain
by Amazon